D1518999

I LOVE GOLDFISH

by Harold T. Rober

BUMBA BOOKS™

LERNER PUBLICATIONS ◆ MINNEAPOLIS

Note to Educators:

Throughout this book, you'll find critical thinking questions. These can be used to engage young readers in thinking critically about the topic and in using the text and photos to do so.

Lerner Publications Company
A division of Lerner Publishing Group, Inc.
241 First Avenue North
Minneapolis, MN 55401 USA

For reading levels and more information, look up this title at www.lernerbooks.com.

Library of Congress Cataloging-in-Publication Data

The Cataloging-in-Publication Data for *I Love Goldfish* is on file at the Library of Congress.
ISBN 978-1-5124-1415-8 (lib. bdg.)
ISBN 978-1-5124-1521-6 (pbk.)
ISBN 978-1-5124-1522-3 (EB pdf)

Manufactured in the United States of America
1 – VP – 7/15/16

Expand learning beyond the printed book. Download free, complementary educational resources for this book from our website, www.lerneresource.com.

Table of Contents

Pet Goldfish

I picked out a goldfish at the pet store.

I will take it home and care for it.

I will watch it swim.

Goldfish need a big tank.

They need room to swim.

I put small rocks in the tank.

The rocks sit at the bottom

of the tank.

**Why might
you put rocks
in a
fish tank?**

I fill the tank with plants.

The goldfish swims

through the plants.

Goldfish like to explore.

Goldfish need clean water.

I have a filter for my tank.

The filter keeps the

water clean.

Why do we need to keep a fish's water clean?

We change some of the water every week.

This keeps our fish healthy.

I use a net to move my goldfish.

Why should you use a net to move goldfish?

Goldfish food looks like little flakes.

I feed my fish two times each day.

I am careful not to give the fish too much food.

Some people get more than

one goldfish.

The fish must be the same size.

Otherwise they may not get along.

A goldfish can live

for twenty years.

It makes a great pet.

Goldfish Supplies

tank

net

food

filter

plant

rocks

Picture Glossary

explore

to move and look around to find new things

filter

a device that cleans water

net

a tool used to catch something in water

tank

a large container for liquid

23

Index

Read More

Brannon, Cecelia H. *Pet Goldfish.* New York: Enslow Publishing, 2017.

Gibbs, Maddie. *Goldfish.* New York: PowerKids Press, 2014.

Kawa, Katie. *Colorful Goldfish.* New York: Gareth Stevens Publishing, 2012.

Photo Credits